Not go away is my name

Also by Alberto Ríos

Poetry

A Small Story about the Sky
The Dangerous Shirt
The Theater of Night
The Smallest Muscle in the Human Body
Teodoro Luna's Two Kisses
The Warrington Poems
The Lime Orchard Woman
Five Indiscretions
Whispering to Fool the Wind
Sleeping on Fists
Elk Heads on the Wall

Fiction

The Curtain of Trees
Pig Cookies
The Iguana Killer

Nonfiction

Capirotada: A Nogales Memoir

Not go away is my name

Alberto Ríos

Copper Canyon Press
Port Townsend, Washington

Cover art: Marisa Takal, *I'm Driving By,* 2019. Oil on canvas, 50 × 65 in. Image courtesy of Night Gallery.

Copper Canyon Press is in residence at Fort Worden State Park in Port Townsend, Washington, under the auspices of Centrum. Centrum is a gathering place for artists and creative thinkers from around the world, students of all ages and backgrounds, and audiences seeking extraordinary cultural enrichment.

LIBRARY OF CONGRESS CATALOGING-IN-PUBLICATION DATA
Names: Ríos, Alberto, author.
Title: Not go away is my name / Alberto Ríos.
Description: Port Townsend, Washington : Copper Canyon Press, [2020]
Identifiers: LCCN 2019056175 | ISBN 9781556595875 (paperback)
Subjects: LCGFT: Poetry.
Classification: LCC PS3568.I587 N68 2020 | DDC 811/.54—dc23
LC record available at https://lccn.loc.gov/2019056175

98765432 FIRST PRINTING

COPPER CANYON PRESS
Post Office Box 271
Port Townsend, Washington 98368
www.coppercanyonpress.org

Acknowledgments

These poems appeared in earlier versions in the following publications:

Academy of American Poets: “Don’t Go into the Library,” “Faithful Forest,” “A House Called Tomorrow”

Academy of American Poets Poem-a-Day: “December Morning in the Desert,” “The Secret in the Mirror”

The Arizona Republic: “Five Years Later”

Cedar Rock: “Immigrant Centuries” (as “Immigrant Times”)

Disquieting Muses Quarterly: “The Adjustments” (as “The Change in Seasons”), “Leaving without Saying Goodbye”

Fifth Wednesday Journal: “The Cactus That Is My Cactus,” “The Sonoran Season,” “Telling the Family Stories”

The Georgia Review: “Industralia,” “The Quiet Boy Noé, Who Waited to Speak,” “The Scorpion of Loud,” “Seahorse in the Desert”

Goodbye, Mexico: Poems of Remembrance: “We Are of a Tribe”

JuxtaProse: “Border Ratings”

The MacGuffin: “Amor Bruto y Azul,” “¡Azúcar!,” “The Barrel Cactuses of the Northern Sonoran Desert,” “The Black Screen,” “Salted Watermelon”

New Letters: “El Trabajo”

Plume: “Muxica”

Poetry: “Even-Keeled and At-Eased”

Poetry Northwest: “Border Boy,” “The Boys and Their Growing,” “I Do Not Go Away,” “The Morning News,” “What Will Not Stay Still Long Enough to Be Named”

Prairie Schooner: “The Cockfight Place”

The Quirk: “The Young Man Frankie Thinks His Secret Thoughts”

Tin House: “Dawn Callers”

Zócalo Magazine: “The Flour Mill Tour,” “This Afternoon Explaining about Changing Things”

Several poems were first performed in the play *Amexica,* by James Garcia and Alberto Ríos.

Thanks to Arizona State University for its abiding support of my work.

For Inés Anita

Welcome, curly-haired little one, welcome and always welcome

Contents

One

Gifts for those who will see them

Two

The day has finished but has not gone easily

Three

Away from this small house on a quiet street

Four

The forest of used-to-be

Five

Look back only for as long as you must

Not go away is my name

One Gifts for those who will see them

¡Azúcar!

1

Celia Cruz opened all her concerts with this solitary word.
Not hello, or welcome, not *ladeez and gennelmen.*

¡Azúcar! A benediction, an invocation, a summary judgment—
All of these, all at once, gathered into that single word,

Sugar. More than its literalness, the word was far eclipsed
By its metaphoric extension: sweetness.

It was a moment of transformation, which was then the evening,
Which was then life itself. It was a worldview

In a half second, forged by the heartfelt, immense, deceptively
Simple invocation of a small word in a big universe.

2

The sugar. It was always there for coffee, for tea and cereal,
This great magician of the kitchen table,

The great family doctor that made almost anything better,
Its cure in tasting, that moment of lightness in triumph over all else.

Sugar was what my great-grandmother could no longer have,
Then my grandmother, then my father.

It was a ghost limb of the mouth for them,
Something they could not forget but kept trying to taste.

What we want, what we hope to give, all of it: so close,
In a small bowl on the kitchen table for our whole lives.

Salted Watermelon

In front of me I have a yellow plastic bowl full of watermelon cubes.
I put salt onto them, trying to avoid making a halo on the TV tray.

Curiously, I have given up table salt in all other things.
This is different, facing the great, green whale of hot summer nights—

This salt is a brazen act of still-wild, desert childhood,
Putting salt on watermelon a way of staying young,

True to the me that once was and still is and will be.
Putting a salted cube of watermelon like this into the mouth—

It's like riding your horse into the rolling hills as fast as you can.
It is a moment of everything, and all you can hope to do is hold on.

Your eyes close hard, you bite down, you prepare to be overwhelmed.
The crush of the melon in the bite of the teeth—

I suspect just even thinking about the watermelon makes my mouth water,
Ready for the thrill of riding the red horse, the bit-in-the-mouth work of it.

But the Dutch-painterly red flesh is itself already all water, and if so am I,
As the scientists say, then I don't know where our oceans meet.

Except for this: they met first in childhood, and I drowned
And it drowned, everything in us given over to the desert's red sea.

Border Boy

I grew up on the border and though I left
I have brought it with me wherever I've gone.

Its line guides me, this long, winding thread of memory.
The border wasn't as big as they say—

It fit neatly behind my eyes and between my ears—
It guides me still, I know, but it is not a compass.

It is not a place out there but a place in here.
I catch on its barbed wire in both places.

It is a line I step over and a ledge I duck under.
I have looked underneath its skirts, and it has caught me—

Many times. We're old friends and we play the game well.
When someone says *border,* now, or *frontera,* or *the line,*

La línea, or *the fence,* or whatever else
We name the edge and the end of things—

I hear something missing in the words,
The *what it all used to be.* Its name does not include its childhood.

I grew up liking the border and its great scar,
Its drama always good for a story the way scars always are.

A scar is the place where the hurting used to be.
A scar the heroic signature of the healed.

The border is not a scar. Instead, it is something we keep picking at,
Something that has no name.

The border I knew was something with a history.
But this thing now, it is a stranger even to itself.

Muxica

The border fence,
The crossing chain links, the twisted wires:

The fence is strung like two harps
At cross-purposes,

Two harps at the same time:
One with its strings up and down,

The other with its strings sideways.
To make music this way

Is difficult. To hear
The song of the two harps

Requires someone ready to play.
We are waiting.

El Trabajo

Where they crossed does not exist on any map.
People will only say that it is impossible.

That boy, Juan, René, Eddie, Raúl—
That boy works to make sure his footprints are erased.

He uses old tire shreds, tying them to his shoes
As if they were skis, sliding instead of stepping.

Being invisible will be his work even after he stops walking.
Being quiet will be his life. Marco, Picho, Ulises.

His mother says, he is a good boy.
He works hard. He has made himself and his family unseen.

However old he becomes, he has done such a good job
No one will ever see him. Paco, Bobby, Moisés,

Thin as wind, gone as fast.
Pablo, Ricardo, Kiki, Nando, Ladislao.

Erasing their movement, he has dragged
An old ocotillo-branch screen

Behind where his family has walked,
Has stopped, has caught what breath there is to catch,

All of it summer fire. Carlos, Flaco, Huicho
Laughs with his mother and his sisters.

They cry, but they laugh harder: It is all so close,
Everything. So close, which is now another way to say *so far.*

Every step taken creates one more step that needs to be taken—
Such are the rules of this world.

A scholar, an architect, a doctor, a race-car driver
At work in the mesquite scrub and hard dark of the desert.

Trumpet player, inventor, teacher, believer: Somewhere,
He will be all of these. Arturo, Memo, Benny, José.

I Do Not Go Away

You have terror and I have tears.
In this cruel way, we are for each other.

We are at war. You always win.
But I do not go away.

You shoot me again. Again, I do not go away.
You shoot with bullets, but you have nothing else.

I fight back. I shoot you
With fragments of childhood, where you played the hero.

I shoot you with memories of your mother
And your little sister, Maritza.

I shoot you with spring in the rolling mountains
And the taste of plantain bananas and sugar.

You do not fall down dead—
You can kill me, where all I can do

Is hold up the mirror of remembering to you—
The mirror of everything you have done.

You set fire to me with gasoline.
I set fire to you with the memory of your first love.

You cut my hands off. I cut your hands off
With the way you saw them disappear

When you were diving into the warm water of the lake,
The summer of swimming with your brother.

Do you remember the names of the left-for-dead?
The damaged, the hounded, the hurt?

Do you remember my name?

Your fist is hard.
My name is crying.

You strike a match.
My name is cringe.

You lift your foot.
My name is pain.

You wake up.
My name is closed eyes.

Your smile mimics the size of the opening
On the side of a head, a crude opening

That a mean needle will stitch up tonight.
Your arm laughs at me with its muscle.

All this. All these tears you have made,
This water you have found in the desert,

All this blood you have drawn
From the bodies of so many who needed it.

You win. You have always won.
All I can do is not go away.

Not go away is my name.

The Morning News

Seasons will not be still,
Filled with the migrations of birds

Making their black script on the open sky,
Those hasty notes of centuries-old goodbyes.

The clouds and the heavens make a memo book,
A diary of it all, if only for a day.

The birds write much, but then rewrite all the time,
News continuous, these small pencil tips in flight.

They are not alone in the day's story.
Jets, too, make their writing on the blue paper—

Jets, and at night, satellites and space stations.
Like it or not, we are all subscribers to the world's newspaper

Written big in the frame of the window in front of us.
Today, we wave to neighborhood riders on horses.

We hear the woodpecker at work on the chimney.
There is news everywhere.

All this small courage,
So that we might turn the page.

Border Ratings

If the ratings for *The Border* would just go down,
We could cancel it. The television and radio

Networks, the newspapers and blogs: they'd have to—
A sound business decision, they'd say. *We had no choice.*

A spirited letter-writing campaign supporting the border show
Might follow, but it wouldn't do much good—the soldiers, the agents,

They all will have gone on to more lucrative roles, accountants,
Mechanics, calendar pinups, heartthrob guest appearances

On other cable television reality shows. The sunglasses,
Jeeps, and guns would have already been shipped over

To the documentary division, happy to get them,
Better able now to tell yesterday's sad story.

The Adjustments

When coffee first arrived in Europe,
It was referred to as "Arabian wine."

In turn-of-the-century San Francisco,
The Bank of America began as the Bank of Italy.

When Cortés arrived at Tenochtitlán on November 8, 1519,
Moctezuma II greeted him warmly and kissed his hand.

All of that. We are amazed by the smallest of things
Coming before us, the facts that seem so strange to us now

As we live in their opposite rooms.
In 1935, reports say, when Isaac Bashevis Singer

Arrived in New York, he was thirty years old
And could speak only three words in English:

"Take a chair."
But then he learned other words. It helped.

Immigrant Centuries

These are immigrant times
And the lines are long,

The signs for jobs few,
The songs sadder, the air meaner.

Everyone is hungry.
Everyone is willing.

Jobs are not jobs but lives lived
Hard at the work of being human.

These are immigrant times,
And the lines are long again.

The Cactus That Is My Cactus

This afternoon, I sit next to a giant cactus—not against it,
No matter how many small plaster statues and black velvet paintings

Say so. On the velvet, that peasant man is not a picture of me,
Not a painting of my brother, nor of anyone else I know. Who is that?

Little man in a big hat with the drooping tips of a large mustache—
He probably fell against the cactus, was stabbed by the thousand needles,

Then died a gruesome death. Apparently, nobody was able to unstick him.
So there he sits, a warning to all. The velvet painting is suddenly clear:

A public service announcement for *Don't do this.*
Not that anyone does.

I can't in fact remember anyone at all sitting against a cactus
In all the years I've lived in the desert. Not any kind of cactus.

But if that man is not me, the cactus in the painting *is* my cactus.
It is a wild and happy saguaro, arms everywhere, exuberant.

My saguaro, that curious Liberace candelabrum, that supplicant,
Arms raised for a century—it should be tired.

But after so long it knows no other way, no other direction
But up. It cannot stop, take a break, have some coffee and a doughnut,

Put its hands in its pockets and walk off for a while
In search of the ice-cream truck.

More statue than tree, more arm than branch,
It is set in the century of its ways.

The hairs on its arms stand up, all the time. Afraid, angry, fierce,
Thrilled—it's hard to say. The saguaro will not speak, or if it does,

It is very quiet. I myself don't want to get so close.
Perhaps what happens is that I miss what it whispers.

But it understands. It takes no offense. Quite the opposite.
With its arms it offers me, regardless,

A bounty of toothpicks, of a sailmaker's needles,
A writer's harvest of exclamation points.

This giant on earth, done with walking, this one
And the rest of its kind making their small town against time.

Giver of gifts for those who will see them:
You and I, cactus, we are clear on the quiet exchanges

The desert makes with its creature citizens.
In passing by, and every time, I never fail to wave,

As every time I see you, you are invariably—*invariably*—
Waving your arms in delight at seeing me.

Dawn Callers

The dawn callers and morning bringers,
I hear them as they intend themselves to be heard,

Quick sonic sparks in the morning dark,
Hard at the first work of building the great fire.

The soloist rooster in the distance,
The cheeping wrens, the stirring, gargling pigeons

Getting ready for the work of a difficult lifetime,
The first screet of the peahen in the far field,

All of it a great tag-of-sounds game engaging even the owls,
The owls with their turned heads and everything else that is animal.

Then, too, the distant thunder of the garbage truck,
That lumbering urban whale.

Through it all, the mourning doves say
There, there—which is to say, everything is all right.

I believe them. They have said this to me ever since childhood.
I hear them. I hear them and I get up.

Two The day has finished but has not gone easily

White among the Colors

The French refer to a drop of milk as *un nuage de lait*—
Literally, a cloud of milk.

Marshmallows, in colloquial Spanish, are called *pedos de monja*—
Nuns' farts. Sorry.

The Chinese character for white derives from *big-bellied*.
It symbolizes the unknown, babies, and ghosts.

White, science tells us, is all colors combined.
In it, therefore, we should expect to see the polychromatic rainbow,

A full artist's palette of used and unused paints and paint shadows.
And we do: We see plain white, plain—

Thrilling, raw, constant color, all the stars all at once,
Untamed pigment taken from the loud high tips of cresting water,

From scream engaged, from sigh delivered.
Color of inside-coconut and side-eye and sand dollar,

Color of the palette all colors sit on,
Waiting for the artist to paint the world.

Everywhere. We see ordinary white, it is true, and fortunate:
This wild ship-sail into the deep water of the hard dark.

The Secret in the Mirror

The mirror is dirty from the detritus of dailiness—
I look in the mirror and am suddenly freckled.

A week out from being cleaned, maybe two, maybe more:
The Milky Way shows itself in the secret silver,

This star chart in my own bathroom,
Aglow not in darkness but with the lights on,

Everything suddenly so clear.
It is not smear I am looking at, but galaxies.

It is not toothpaste and water spots—
When I look in the mirror, it is writing and numbers,

Musical notes, ones and zeros, Morse-like codes, runes.
I am looking over into the other side,

And over there, whoever they are, it turns out
They look a lot like me. Like me, but freckled.

I Did It

My dreams lean constantly criminal, incorrigibly illegal—
They hold fast to no laws,

They will not be measured 9 to 5, much less minute to minute.
They wander where they will and see what they want.

No job, no carnival mirror, no ostrich interests them for long.
They speed down the highway at 100, veering suddenly left,

Laughing, without apology, not always actually in a car.
I have dreamt myself in just this way—me of so many names.

I, whoever I am, who am not who I was
The night before, who am not who I will be tomorrow

As I make my way from pillow to wherever it is we go,
Ringing the bell on the door to the mansion of dreams.

In that dark abode, all things are possible and happen:
The egg is a hammer; the nose is a planet.

Whatever might be done, I have done.
Whatever might be seen, I have seen, and did not turn away.

This is where I go.
When I wake, I try not to tell the world where I have been.

The Circus Act Man

Some men are not men at all.
They are a clever compendium of boys

Situated one on top of the other
Each with his own set of thoughts

Brought along from the age that he was
When he took position.

Each one wants to move wherever
He wants to move, and often does.

It is all a simple truth: everyone knows
The little boy never leaves the man,

That the good intentions of the sweet boy
Not yet a teenager stay resident,

Making him want to be the hero,
Sorrowing inconsolably at the dying of his dog.

Then himself the teenager takes over,
Demanding more room, wanting

So much but without a name to summon it.
Finally, one gets past all this, head up

As if from a deep dive, lifting himself
Out of and away from the water,

Ready to get dressed and go to dinner
And lead a regular life.

So many boys. So many sets of ears,
So many eyes, so much breath taken in—

All of them inside together, not strangers
But not precisely friends.

The Feeling of Feeling

It happens everywhere, all the time.
Sometimes it is a birdcall, the plaintive

Mating urge made loud and larger than the bird itself,
That sound big as the centuries that have kept it

Alive in the fiber of the bird. A birdcall—
Then nothing, its echo or its resonance all that is left,

A birdcall as if it were a stone thrown into a lake—
Something ripples out and goes on, but it is not the stone.

Sometimes, the feeling is rain falling onto the desert,
A flash flood so suddenly there then so suddenly gone,

Alive, though, in its telling for the towns that have lived it,
Alive in the story of itself: so brown, big, so Tasmanian devil.

Sometimes, what we feel is simple hunger,
Its gnawing made to go away at first by food,

Its fullness lasting for a good while, until
The hunger wolf returns, ravenous again for anything,

The wolf making itself at home, coming back every day
To lie down next to the blood it knows is there inside us.

It is a feeling. There are other things. Music comes and goes,
The sound of a trumpet, bagpipes, a simple whistle in the distance.

Light goes dark but will be light again at the flipping of a switch.
We go away. The dog so sadly dies. But then there is

Someone else, and a new dog. We are gone as our parents
But we are there as our children.

We are a long list of all these moments,
Each feeling everything in its time.

Legacies

The bearer of extra strings
For those that break.

Some footprints make noise and are loud—
Walking where they like,

Stepping over everything heel-first.
They are the bagpipes of walking,

The accordions, the Roman trumpets,
The bugler's rooster-call to reveille.

But some footprints are quiet—
Walking where they're needed,

Always welcome, the sound of rain
In the desert of desperate need,

Footprints so soft we rarely hear them,
Leaving no scratching sound to the ear.

But what is quiet is also strongest
In that it does not walk away,

Nor is its stance in front, or behind,
But by one's side, able to be counted on

Even and especially through the wild
Noises of the dark. In this we are given

The lullaby, the étude, one's simple hum,
The double bass of it all, the contrabassoon,

The long, sustained note rising from an oboe,
The music underneath music, the work

Underneath work: The great gift that—all along—
Something magnificently quiet has been the song.

Don't Go into the Library

The library is dangerous—
Don't go in. If you do

You know what will happen.
It's like a pet store or a bakery—

Every single time you'll come out of there
Holding something in your arms.

Those novels with their big eyes and wagging tails.
Those no-nonsense, all-muscle Dobermans,

All nonfiction and business,
Cuddly when they're young,

But then the first page is turned and no turning back.
And those sleek, fast, beautiful greyhounds: poems.

The doughnut scent of it all, *knowledge,*
The aroma of coffee being made

In all those books, something for everyone,
The deli offerings of civilization itself.

The library is the book of books,
Its concrete and wood and glass covers

Keeping within them the very big,
Very long story of everything.

The library is dangerous, full
Of answers. If you go inside,

You may not come out
The same person who went in.

When the World Speaks Back to Us, Many Years Later

I am holding a piece of paper whose corner is curling up.
I tap at it, but it does not want to stay flat.

It does not want to do what the other bottom corner is doing.
To hold it down, I put my thumb on it more firmly, impatiently,

Expecting it to stay. As I raise my thumb, however,
The corner of the paper immediately comes up with it.

The motion is so stark it seems a signal to me, a shout—
Something in that quadrant trying to speak to me,

To wave, to beckon me closer with this motion.
I am no fool and do not take the bait—

This may be a joke. I remember that high-school thing we used to do
In the library: We would use a pencil to tightly roll up

The due-date slips of paper glued to the inside of a book cover. Then
We would unroll them, close the book, and put it on the front counter.

When the librarian opened the book, the slip would curl up suddenly,
Making the razzing sound of a rude, rude tongue.

The librarian would look around, eyes narrowed, no laughter.
The laughter belonged to us, but we were smart enough to wait—

In the hallway, the joke was ours. We threw it back and forth like a football.
We savored it for days and now years with this telling.

Today, this piece of paper I am holding, terribly, calls me to account.
It will not lie flat.

This is only a Thursday morning. Every day, each hour, so clearly—
I am surrounded by all the smallest things I have ever done.

A Quiet Evening in August

It is dusk. Earth eats the dragon.
The singed edges of sky orange,

Fire in red smoke plumes everywhere,
Lavender, finally, lavender and gray

The great bruise of the moment in the sky,
Weak yellow smudges framing the end.

The day has finished but has not gone easily—
If color were noise

We would have thought it our end as well.
Instead, we sit to dinner inside the house,

And take no notice, darkness becoming so simply
Our personal and the world's dessert.

Three Away from this small house on a quiet street

Five Years Later

I was, and now I am.
So much goes into the saying of those few words.

Sometimes this change is sweetness,
A kiss, a caress. Sometimes,

Nothing warns us. It cannot be thought by us.
It is done to us. A gun,

An earthquake, a flood—any of the muscular
Horrors of this world.

In those instances, we don't ask for it,
We don't get to take a deep breath,

It is simply the end of the chapter
And page 1 of the next. We are thrown

Into the deep water and we are angry,
We are angry, we are angry.

We could not swim, but now we are swimming—
We have to swim.

It is not fair. It is never fair.
We have no chance to be part of the decision

That changes us.
We were, and then we are. Regrettably,

We are not alone. If it is one of us,
It is all of us, so many of us.

We were, and now we are.
Sweetness or cruelty, suddenness, shock,

A rough touch that could be either:
We are changed.

If it has been a kiss, our lives are turned powerfully
Toward lightness.

But when it is not sweetness, not a kiss,
We live the rest of our lives as someone else,

But someone who is still us.
If we had a gun, because we did have a gun,

If things had gone differently, better,
If the rehab had been more effective,

Had God stepped in, had anyone heard:
We would be living in the regular world.

We could look at the rabbits along the highway
And the blue, ragged mountains in the distance

Like anyone.
But five years after something has happened to us

We are not the *anyone.*
The jackrabbits and the Tucson Mountains—

We love them, not easily but fiercely, fiercely
In the new way we have had to find.

We love them as who we are now.
We love because that's what's left.

The Scorpion of Loud

In the place between scorpions and manners,
Between scream and please pass the salt,

Somewhere between John Kennedy's November
And my next-door neighbor's blue flowerbeds,

We live our lives.
If we're lucky, no one will notice us.

Of course, we think we want it not to be like that:
We think we want to be noticed.

We want to be famous, handsome, spontaneous—
We want to be rich. We want to be good dancers,

Alive and at ease in the rhythms of the tango. We want
To be brain surgeons, astronauts, race-car drivers, movie stars—

Parnelli Jones, Roberto Clemente, Howard Hughes, John Glenn.
We want to be like that. Like them and a few more.

But if you *are* them, Wonder Woman, if you are the headline,
If everyone stands and applauds—

If you do all this, understand as well what comes next:
The Scorpion of Loud is out there, stinger

So curiously shaped like a question mark—
Stinger poised at the ready.

The Flour Mill Tour

Ed—that was his name, on the tag—
Ed himself, our guide, was a ghost, flour

Faintly on his face, under his eyes,
White in the creases of his white uniform,

Giving him the aspect of an undertaker
In Heaven, someone from the movies,

And with his grumbling voice,
He was the static, the snow scrambling

Old television shows. This man,
He was a photographic negative—white

Under his fingernails, this place's
Sign of hard work, white and not black,

But filthy, caught onto him everywhere—
Opposite and the same as a coal miner,

Each working their days in dust.
Not from it and not to it, but in it.

This Afternoon Explaining about Changing Things

This afternoon, after lunch, I will listen to a man read his story to me.
He has no one else. His wife died several years ago—and it's all wrong:

He never got to read it to her as her death is what started him writing.
It's earnest, and a part of my own life now this afternoon.

His face as he reads, his hunger to hear that I've heard what he's said,
The gravity, the brave shoulders, the weight, the pauses.

His conversation on these afternoons is a little too fast, that nervousness,
His wanting to get it right, to know the rules, to color inside the lines.

What else is there, after all, for him—if this is how he sees it, and he does.
This is the gift she has left to him, and what he might give to her still.

This man is older, not a formal student, not in a class, but someone
Who has taken the time to make an appointment and come to see me.

We share the same first name, which is always curious between people.
It's an immediate connection, self-evident, even when nobody says so.

Of course I want to write these words for him. I want to tell him how.
My love, I would start, and perhaps finish there as well.

But he says more to her, always more. *I'm waiting for you to come home—*
Or else, *tell me where you are and I'll come and pick you up.*

That's what he wants to say. *I'm waiting for you. Come home.*
I believe it all, every word he stumbles over. I don't like the words,

I don't like that they affect me—they are a beginner's sentimental lament.
I want to cover it up for him in better language, and I try to show him

How. How to do it. He is smart, old-world smart: from South America,
The traditions of poem and celebration and gift.

But he never seems to be able to change anything, never seems
To understand what I have explained to him. Finally, I am grateful for this.

He moves a few words around to please me, something here and there,
But not very much. The next time I see him and we go over the story again,

Nothing has changed.
That's how much those words mean.

I want to change what cannot be changed,
Not by me, not by him.

This is what he teaches me, and I thank him each time
For these long afternoons in which I listen.

Amor Bruto y Azul

1

I love you with every sharp edge
Of every broken piece of

My tender and hard-brittled heart—
So many edges, so much love,

So many broken shards.
You make my skin young. You make my blood old.

But there you are, in everything.
I love you with all the broken pieces of my heart.

You. Even when I love you
You make me angry. I find ways to fight you—

I hit you with my eyes—
I ball them into two fists and strike.

But you take them.
You only grow with the brute force of my big eyes—

They put more of something into you.
Those fists, those eyes, you hold them.

Then in time, slowly, you open them, relax them.
You show me my hands as if new again,

My hands which are my eyes.
We artists.

2

When I speak, your name comes out of my mouth.
You are my words.

It's not that I want to speak you—
It's that you are inside me—not just sometimes,

But all the time.
When I open my mouth, I can't help it—

I open my mouth and you come out of me.
My legs run away from you so far, so fast,

To the ends of this blue earth,
So that I am suddenly behind you, chasing you.

I circle away and toward you.
My magnet, my opposite, my love.

You are my necklace.
I am the bristles of all your brushes.

3

A parade of spiders across your brow.
A bridge of spiders across a river of tears.

Small legs, small hairs, small brushstrokes,
Your brow is the path through the jungle.

Your brow is the dark arco iris,
The rainbow absent of all color.

You gave its color to your painting,
Even in your darkest brushstrokes.

4

I felt as if in painting your face,
So large in my imagination, so much of you,

I stumbled and fell off the ladder.
As I fell, my brush slipped wildly

And left this black rainbow of my falling on your face,
Over your eyes. This is my story.

You saw me fall and you held me with those eyes,
Those hands. You kept me to you.

All this drama.
We should have been novels instead of artists.

5

There are no straight lines between us.
Everything is a curved and crooked path,

Through blue, through dark red,
Heavy gray through a canvas sea.

A path inside the sea—
That's us.

6

I see you here and then over there, on the ceiling,
Through the window,

You and your reflection and your laugh without mouth—
That look you have, that sad laughter

That comes more from the mouth of your brow
Than the mouth we think of. Nothing is easy.

To speak from there, that second mouth, as you do—
Nothing is easy.

And I am the one who painted it there.
I am the one who made you keep it there,

Passionate in its *yes,* furious in its *no,*
Bored with anything in between.

7

That singular brow-line across the tops of my eyes,
It's a dare.

Make sure you want me to see what you have to show
Before you cross it.

Make sure my seeing is worth the trouble honesty will cause.
I have kept your thin mustache where you left it,

Those scraggly strands of yours, those passions,
I have kept them where you kissed me,

That hair that was yours
For a moment on my forehead between my brows.

That thin mustache, that moment of you,
I have not been able to let it go.

I keep it with me, I wear it,
I keep it in front of me as if I am thinking it.

8

Your mouth on my eyes,
That's why I see darkness.

You meant it as a kiss,
And another kiss, but it turned to

Me drowning in what you had to say,
How absolutely you said it,

Me swimming in your breath,
Trying with all my strength to reach a shore.

But the truth is, in that darkness I stay where I am.
I drown all the time. I get used to it.

9

Those small strands of hair between my brows,
They are the bristles of my brushes.

I look through paintbrushes
At life. I look through paint

To see what's there. To see best,
I close my eyes.

Even-Keeled and At-Eased

I have contracted. I have eased
Gwendolyn Brooks, “the mother”

But the truth is, I am Thursday on a Monday. I
Am the walking calendar alive of mixed-up days and dim hours. I have

A week inside me, a week or a year, time out of order. I have contracted
With the world to behave, to try, hard, to be Monday on a Monday. I

Look like I am happiness, don’t you think? On Monday, to you I have
The right laugh, and seem always to be even-keeled and at-eased.

The Black Screen

There is no color in the color black, no hue, no shading—
Black is the absence of color, yet we give it a color's name.

Black is to color what zero is to numbers.
It should be invisible. But we cannot help ourselves:

We see it everywhere. It has followed us through the centuries
In its sinuous cloak of night and thunderous sky,

In watermelon seeds and skunk fur, in obsidian blades and Apache tears,
In death, and even, finally, into the smallest box of Crayolas,

Perched beak of a crow in the branches of a polychrome forest.
We see it and we see with it, black present in the center of the eye.

Everything fades to it. Cancer is made from it. Black is a limousine.
Black is not black. It is not nothing, not invisible, not without.

It is something, and its something is cousin to the depths inside us.
Through the centuries it has come to mean many things,

It has swaddled evening and lent its name to human skin.
Champion of the shadows and keeper of the room behind closed eyes,

It tries to be unseen but we recognize it everywhere.
It suffers itself as velvet to the garish liking of the border tourist.

Black, finally, the color or lack of color, is simply black, exhausted
Journeyman in thankless service to the imagination of all things.

December Morning in the Desert

The morning is clouded and the birds are hunched,
More cold than hungry, more numb than loud,

This crisp Arizona shore, where desert meets
The coming edge of the winter world.

It is cold news in stark announcement,
The myriad stars making bright the black,

As if the sky itself had been snowed upon.
But the stars—all those stars—

Where does the sure noise of their hard work go?
These plugs sparking the motor of an otherwise quiet sky,

Their flickering work everywhere in a white vastness:
We should hear the stars as a great roar

Gathered from the moving of their billion parts, this great
Hot-rod skid of the Milky Way across the asphalt night,

The assembled, moving glints and far-floating embers
Risen from the hearth-fires of so many other worlds.

Where does the noise of it all go
If not into the ears, then hearts of the birds all around us,

Their hearts beating so fast and their equally fast
Wings and high songs,

And the bees, too, with their lumbering hum,
And the wasps and moths, the bats, the dragonflies—

None of them sure that any of this is going to work,
This universe—we humans oblivious,

Drinking coffee, not quite awake, calm and moving
Into the slippers of our Monday mornings,

Shivering because, we think,
It's a little cold out there.

Industralia

Tape measure from its room goes out only so far then fast as it can runs back again.
One day it will meet the vacuum cleaner cord and they will run away together.

Beautiful paper clip, what's left of King Minos's vast treasure, his silver labyrinth:
Confusion attaching itself to everything in the mysterious shape of organization.

Stapler, hiding alligator, swamp beast in a nice suit, alligator that has gone to college,
Lurking on the desktop innocuously, quietly, but ready in an instant with its teeth.

Eraser, perched atop its yellow lifeguard stand, looking over the bay of literature
Into the ocean of all writing, ready to save writers from drowning in themselves.

Flashlight, ancient lighthouse at its work still, keeping the big ships in the storm
Away from this small house on a quiet street.

Back scratcher, delicate leg of a sleeping greyhound dog, urgent leg
Borrowed from that moment in the dream when the chase for the rabbit has begun.

Rubber band, rubber band, easily smiling, smiling wider—stretched
So happy on some days its embrace extends all the way around me.

Small fan, outboard motor of this dry-dock world, spinning as if to make
A start of this desk, sailing us—goodbye, goodbye—to the island of Very Far Away.

Four The forest of used-to-be

What Will Not Stay Still Long Enough to Be Named

Today is a cool-weather day, curious for middle spring, usually so hot
Already, the desert taking off its great winter coat with a flourish.

We focus our attention on the strange bird in the jacaranda tree.
The bird is probably not strange—we simply know little about birds,

Their names, their habits, their habitats. We hear them often enough,
We recognize their songs but never remember the lyrics. We lack

The strength of memory that would make us able to say *mockingbird*
Loudly, fully certain, and in a manner that would make people think

We could recognize other mockingbirds. We've lived our whole lives here,
We've learned the names of so much around us a hundred times over—

Still, nothing sticks. Tourists and friends always ask, and often know
More than we do—what kind of bird is that, what kind of cactus, what kind of smell?

The next thing is, of course, what's the best restaurant, the best bakery, best hike.
This is the same litany of questions every time, and I shrug at all of them.

I don't know, I confess. I've lived here too long and everything changes, I think.
It is, instead, the moments I look to, so fleeting, so perfect, so many—

The first bite of birria and corn tortilla, the jacaranda whenever it blooms, the yellow
Everything of the paloverdes, their fallen thousand happy yellow pieces of light,

The plantains fried in sugar that you can only get at home now. *The best*
Fills this place, so much of it, but always only for a moment, no names adequate

To capture it, naming instead only its memory, or the hope of its recurring.
The vocabulary of what is good here is, finally, a momentary dictionary,

This constant act of discovery, we Magellans and de Anzas of the instant.
That tree? we are asked. *I don't know what it's called today,* we say.

Telling the Family Stories

We pinches of salt—
We tell our family's stories best

By adding something to them.
Hearing about Don Margarito

In a story told a thousand different ways
By a hundred different cousins,

Which story is the real one?
There are so many, and we have listened to them all.

We sprigs of rosemary—afterward,
We do not report the story, as an outsider might.

We do not sit at the table and wait for the meal.
We ourselves tell one more different story among them all,

Having heard what we heard the way we heard, interrupted
By coffee, which then finds its way into our version.

This way we get our stories. We listen while stirring.
We chilies, we family, we are always

At the kitchen table, not in the dining room.
We all bring something to the table later in the day.

We all follow the recipes
Nobody ever wrote down.

Don Margarito's story, and Doña Cuquita's,
They are always new, which is why they can be told

So many times. We leaves of mint,
We do not follow the measure for sugar written down.

Instead, we taste the story of the broken arm we talk about—
All of us cooks, all of us right, all of it true.

CoffeeTea

Coffee is drinking a little bit of ourselves when we were younger.
Tea makes round what at first was square.

Tea hums its way through the otherwise quiet world.
Coffee is brewed from all the black notes on a sheet of fast music.

Coffee is made of old pianos.
Tea is made of Parisian watercolors.

Tea is the palm of the hand.
Coffee always raises its hand in answer to a question.

Coffee is the expansive night sky.
Tea is the quiet turned-earth in the makings of a new garden.

Tea is the audience that has come to watch the actors.
Coffee is the actor who is the undeniable star of the evening.

Coffee shouts; tea whispers.
I drink coffee, but I remember tea.

The Cockfight Place

After they had married, Mariquita one night
Looking for Adolfo went out and found him.

She had to step over a dried phlegm-and-dirt floor
In a dark cockfighting barn, had to step over

A ground made of decades-old sputum
Gifted carelessly from half-shaved, thick men

Everywhere, and dying or just barely living cocks,
A floor bloodgiven, scuffed

Into an inexpert, misshapen setting of scab tiles.
Her husband was drunk, and here.

Mariquita collected Adolfo and took him away
From what he needed to be taken away from.

They would never speak of this night again—
Though for Mariquita the sounds of the fight would not go,

The sounds of all those men huddled,
The odor of the cloying perfume they made on that hot night,

All of them together and shouting, placing bets, spilling beer.
Mariquita remembered, as she made her way past the rooster fight,

How she had seen the one soul-white cock
Spattered with blood like hot kitchen grease.

This cock had an eye pulled fully out
But it continued to fight,

Then lost the other eye to a beak and a hard pull.
Still, it continued to fight, could not stop fighting,

Stretching its head and neck up higher, then higher still,
Trying to see, imagining that something must be blocking its view,

Trying to see, never for a moment thinking it was blind,
Confident that the cheering was its new eyes,

That the noise was sudden muscle.
Both owners kept spraying their fighter birds,

Watering them from their mouths, through their teeth,
Spitting a mist on the fury of the birds,

Fooling them into momentary coolness, until the winner,
The not-white one, finished, allowed itself

To be corralled and soothed and rewarded,
And the owner, laughing through his half beard,

In that old way of these fights, took the cock's head
Into his mouth, that fastest way of cooling an animal best.

At the Recreo and Pitíc

After church in the warm and quiet days along the border,
Sunday afternoons were given over to the tradition of the botana,

Botana, the word, translates in the dictionary as "snack,"
But that's not what it means to those who lived it.

The botana itself was indeed a collection of snacks,
A miscellaneous bit of this and some of that,

Some salsa, some homemade red-brown hot sauce, some
Bites of tamale wrapped in banana leaf from the south, some

Rounds of fried plantain sprinkled with sugar
In the style of the carnivals and circuses.

But the afternoons were not really about the food.
What it all amounted to was an excuse to gather at the bars,

To go where you did not go on other days.
All this and a respectful amount of beer, the A-1,

The Carta Blanca, Dos Equis, the Bohemia and Superior.
It was a quiet chance for wives to see where their husbands went

On Thursday evenings, a chance for husbands to see
What other men did who were not yet married, for children

To see it all, a bright light shone behind the swinging doors
Of a loud bar where on any other day you did not ask.

Even on Sunday afternoon, those places had a curious, cool,
Deep smell emanating from somewhere past those swinging doors.

That smell: that hundred years of spilled beer
And conversation about women.

Baseball on the Mexican Border

Baseball in the fifties was a fever on the border,
Semipro leagues in bloom all over Sonora—

The Tomateros, the tomato growers,
The back-and-forth of the desertlands championship,

The battle of bats between big families in small places,
The Ostioneros de Guaymas, the Naranjeros de Hermosillo—

The oyster workers and the orange growers,
The Cañeros de Los Mochis, los Yaquis de Obregón—

Though everybody's favorite team was always American,
The Pittsburgh Pirates, so far was the reach of Roberto Clemente.

In those days, Tucson was baseball, American baseball,
The spring training home of two memorable teams,

Who were, in those years, the terrible terrible Cleveland Indians
And the horrible horrible Chicago Cubs.

They would, several times during spring training,
Send teams down to the border at Nogales for exhibition games.

They were big news, the only news, the best news.
One spring in the late fifties, it occurred to civic officials

They should gather up all the town's kids
Then send them to a game for free.

The bleachers would be full,
Certainly encouraging the teams to come back.

What nobody knew then was that each team had B and C squads
And this is who they sent

So that the terrible terrible and horrible horrible teams
Were even more terrible and more horrible.

We kids watched and, as I remember it well, we laughed.
Perhaps sending these squads should have been seen as an insult

To the town, to the kids, to baseball itself—
But this event was, instead, something else.

The Tacuarineros de Culiacán and the Mayos de Navojoa:
They were much better than these Cubs and Indians.

I was much better. I thought: *I can do what these guys are doing.*
What might have been an insult was instead an encouragement,

An inspiration. We were so close to those players in our good seats,
So close we saw ourselves out on that field.

The Boys and Their Growing

They run, they run, even when they walk they run.
Seeing the boys hard at work in their various contentments,

Their simple movements, then at last sitting to sun themselves
In small plastic chairs, having watched their grandfather and now

So grandfatherly themselves, but not for long—
Getting up and running again, playing at swords and knights,

Playing at what their grandfather had once played at,
Though he had given them no instruction—

Bird and cat, rocket and moon, everything possible
Inside the walls of this yard,

This yard, which holds in its grass palm the history of this house.
These boys, they will grow and go on to their lives.

All this movement will not show itself on any map,
Will not be recorded in the deed when the house is sold,

But this is where their lives went, in more than equal measure,
Up and down, jumping, skidding and turning, running and falling.

The Young Man Frankie Thinks His Secret Thoughts

Death makes a pretty good lunch, I think. Death, or rather, funerals.
That is, when somebody dies, the rest of us get to eat.

It is sad all right, a sad day, but nobody scrimps on the food.
The people who visit to say they're sorry buy the things you always wondered about—

Those shrimp platters in store windows, shrimp on lettuce beds, red sauce
Right there, right in the middle, neat and handy. It is the opposite of home—

Home is where you might have some shrimp, maybe some big shrimp,
But always right on the day nobody told you the red sauce ran out weeks ago.

It happens every time. You're left pounding on the upside-down, empty bottle,
The separated sauce droplets coming out a little black and stuck together.

At funerals, things are different. Everything is there—shrimp and red sauce both,
Lemons, too, all these things being very thoughtful, even the big, blue cloth napkins.

Fancy tongue sandwiches and family-recipe cilantro salsas and olives and pecans.
And everybody there is personally concerned that you should have it all,

Even though you are just a visitor. *Eat up, son,* they say. They say it repeatedly.
It is curious how you seem to be everybody's son on these occasions.

They don't want you to just eat a little, either—*Look at that ham.*
Have some more, they say. *There's plenty.* And they mean it.

That's what's left to do at a funeral—make sure people get their fill.
There's nothing else left, once all the food is there and the people have arrived.

That's the business of it all. Anything else comes later. Missing a person,
That takes a while. It's not something you have to worry about now.

Nobody else is hungry, so I come prepared. It never fails. People can be counted on
At times like these. I tell you, it always turns out to be my lucky day.

Breakfast That Will Be Mine

The ocean—grand cow of the four horizons—
Chews its cud with soft jaws of wave, patient.

The ocean dines on the world at will. The desert, too,
Is alive with its breakfast, mouse to owl. The mountains,

Complicit in this scheme, grow in their pine humus
A delicatessen's worth of moist choices,

So many beetles, so many old and tired, weak birds,
Small beasts in evidence everywhere at their wilding

But now barely alive, with their accountable wounds:
They will be mine, one day. They will be in my oatmeal—

They will have decayed and become earth
Out of which will grow the things I eat.

In this way they will be in my oatmeal,
Then in my turn one day I will be in theirs.

It is a bargain we make,
A take-turns game, centuries in the playing:

Our good dinner, our big breakfast, the smell of coffee,
These moments in the mouth, this taste of us all.

Beer That Had the Look of Champagne

In those days, the bars were bars for men alone,
It's true, but on some days and at some hours

They were for families, too,
For curious children who could not get enough

Peanuts, peanuts offered open-air to the world,
The peanuts alive and crowded in their little bowls,

Full themselves of conversation, words
Having dropped onto them heavily enough

To keep them from dancing.
The peanuts were next to the glass rings on the tables,

The stains upon stains of beers that had foamed
Around and over glasses, marks happy and old,

Stained into the tabletops like a child's penmanship practice.
The bottles, the glasses, the occasional stray droplets,

They were all different-sized, however, so that together
All the moons, all the planets, and all the suns of the galaxy

Showed themselves on that table to the imaginations of boys,
Boys who were instructed to sit still and be quiet.

The beer in the glasses is what everyone else paid attention to,
Anyway, all the time, every day, Sunday or not.

The old men, the men who sat at the bar exclusively,
Never at the tables, they put salt in their beers each time

Before they lifted a glass,
So that for the few seconds the salt took to descend

The beer had the look of champagne.
The gesture was from the old days, to take down the sediment,

The impurities still floating in the beer,
The beer perhaps not strained as scrupulously as one should.

Whatever happened on other days, for those few moments
Rich champagne brewed from the imagination,

Champagne that no one could afford, champagne
Together with simple table peanuts. Life was good.

Small Detective in a Quiet Kitchen

Lemon squeezer, I met you at a business meeting for the first time—
You were successful, let me say, in trying to impress me with your handshake.

Napkin, you are paper now, but you come from a fine history of linen and circumstance,
Your grandmother in the bosom pocket of a queen and the back pocket of a workman.

Knife, everyone talks about your edginess, not sure what to make of you.
But, come here. You are flat side and good use, reformed criminal, friend so often.

Potato peeler, tough guy, two knives perfectly wielded, biding your time.
It's potatoes today, and sometimes carrots, but with you, anything, anything is possible.

Colander, helmet after a ferocious battle whose head you could not save, bullet holes
Everywhere. Even so, you are now peace itself, the steel plowshare made from sword.

Rolling pin, trying so hard to fix the world, to turn it back, to find its perfect childhood,
To make the world a single dimension, absent the complex, no bumps, a smooth home.

Big bowl, you are the ocean itself, your rim the best beach in the world—in you swim
The great whale potatoes, blowfish peas, carrot eels—place of strange familiars.

Skewer, cousin so clearly in the family tree of nails and needles and javelins, swords,
Toothpicks and lightning rods, for centuries you have helped me and scared me both.

Ladle, big dipper borrowed from the night sky, when I hold you holding soup,
The rice is so suddenly unmasked as what it really is, stars alive in the great water.

Tongs, steel robot hands, you have saved my tender relationship with bacon.
You let me touch the untouchable and hold directly the estranged heart of pure desire.

Cheese grater, metal handkerchief, on your sides you collect so many teardrops and scars,
Catalogue them so carefully, work them in the rough business of helping us to go on.

Spoon, you are the cupped hand made ready for the mouth, the translation of the world
From all of it to what is yours, lifted gracefully in a century that acts otherwise.

Fork, you are made from a landscape of cypress trees, tines straight up, small pitchfork
Bringing down to us the sky itself, that blue on the tongue, that firmament-filled mouth.

Can opener, your detective heart always searching to expose the underlying truth—you
Turn, turn, and turn until the cover is blown, its truth to the world at last revealed.

The Sonoran Season

It's hotter and there's less rain.
I say that every year, and it is said to me in turn.

It used to be cooler by now, my body says.
Instead, November starts the engine of coolness

In the low desert, not September, not October,
Which have become doctors' waiting rooms,

All of us hoping to get better soon,
To recover from the fevers and delirium of summers

That go on for years inside months,
Heat that changes the measures of time itself:

Heat, after all, makes a thing expand.
Heat makes the clock melt.

And when the cool does come, when
The early mornings are chilly, are crisp,

When the evenings require long pants,
A pullover piece of clothing with a zipper,

We laugh. The coolness touches something
Inside us, something from childhood.

I remember being cold, we say.
We say, *I had a pair of gloves once.*

Weak Day

Through the distance in the June heat, the air quivers,
The day itself appearing insubstantial and uncertain in its theater.

A driver seeing this on the highway calls it a mirage,
The strange way the canvas of distance melts.

But something else is at work,
Because how could it not be?

Day wants to be day but has been day so much
It is tired of its actor's lines, sweating in its costume in the desert.

It just wants to go home today. In this heat,
Day is sleepy and can barely keep its eyes open,

So that everything swoons, is barely there, only maybe there,
Day weak in its muscles and feverish at its job.

It needs a day off. It should not have come to work today.
But a call in to the cloud factory went unanswered.

Days-off past were already used and days-off to come were precious.
So, no, today day took its turn, bravely, if with sighs,

But how many more of these could be borne, this theater of cruelty,
This was Subject #1 on the agenda of the Town Council of the Desert.

The cactuses would be there, saying that they, too, found it hard to stand
So long, and the tortoises would chime in with their per diem complaints,

Maybe now everyone understanding that they were not padded.
It simply took a long time, all of this, a very long time for everything.

Day's attorney would be there and would maybe get a hearing this time
Amid the shouts, *A raise, a raise for everything in the desert.*

Faithful Forest

Petrified Forest National Park, Arizona

1

I will wait, said wood, and it did.
Ten years, a hundred, a thousand, a million—

It did not matter. Time was not its measure,
Not its keeper, nor its master.

Wood was *trees* in those first days.
And when wood sang, it was *leaves,*

Which took flight and became birds.

2

It is still forest here, the forest of *used-to-be.*
Its trees are the trees of memory.

Their branches—so many tongues, so many hands—
They still speak a story to those who will listen.

Looking without listening, you will not hear the trees.
You will see only hard stone and flattened landscape,

But if you're quiet, you will hear them.

3

The leaves liked the wind, and went with it.
The trees grew more leaves, but wind took them all.

And then the bare trees were *branches,* which in their frenzy
Made people think of so many ideas—

Branches were lines on the paper of sky,
Drawing shapes on the shifting clouds

Until everyone agreed that they saw horses.

4

Wood was also the keeper of fires.
So many people lived from what wood gave them.

The cousins of wood went so many places
Until almost nobody was left here—that is the way

Of so many families. But wood was steadfast
Even though it was hard from loneliness. Still,

I will wait, said wood, and it did.

Five Look back only for as long as you must

The Jazz of Us

It's not jazz so much as moving to the left or the right of a thing,
Most especially yourself—moving against the compass

That keeps us straight up-and-down, the careful compass needle
Turned suddenly into a game of spin the bottle

One Tuesday night. For one night, the compass points to something
We have not done and will not do again, finding us passage

On a one-time voyage to an unmapped place. Our Tuesday changes.
Next Tuesday or last Tuesday is not this Tuesday.

Today is the Brigadoon of Tuesdays. It is finding the one breath
That can never be found again the same way on another night.

That Tuesday. You had to be there.
Even when we remember, it is new every time, all the time:

And new is shiny, never previously owned, everything working.
It's why, after their best, the great rockers smashed their guitars

At the end of a performance—it would never get better than this.
It's like the crabapples you ate as a kid

That you'll never taste again—apples don't grow the same apple
From seed, but from cuttings. That happiness and that sadness both:

I ate the apples and loved them. Sad that I can't taste them again,
Happy that I did, most of my life dancing in between.

The Nanas and the Tatas

1

One year the nanas and the tatas got together.
It was a Thursday in February, too cold

Really, so that it was hard to see them
Girdled among the blankets, throws and shawls,

Red suspenders and white socks.
It was the residents' regular weekly meeting,

But nothing began until after the first half hour,
Which was taken up with the assembling of their coffees,

Their teas, and their broths, all temperatures just right,
If different for each. As sugars and creams settled, everyone spoke,

But nobody could hear anyone else well enough to understand.
Instead, everyone heard what they wanted.

The whole room was pleased.
The senior center Social Director was especially pleased.

2

But then, with the help of a well-meaning college-student volunteer,
Talk of developing a website came up,

Though nobody quite knew what one was.
The meeting had been informal at first,

A regular day in a regular week
Like any other and so many at the senior center,

But now, today felt more like a Saturday on a Tuesday
In a good way, not a medicine way.

The day felt new. A website! People listening to us!
Everyone who had been speaking now spoke louder.

Canes were raised. Doilies fell to the floor and were wrinkled.
Curiously, everyone was rather pleased instead of irritated—

Action! That's what they wanted, after all,
Though each of them thought of it differently.

3

So many ideas on how to better run the world:
Finally and concisely, *I don't like spiders,* said Clotilde,

Loudest of all so that everyone could hear—
Not because her voice was loud but because she so rarely spoke

So that all their ears grew bigger to listen in that moment:
I was always brushing the black-widow webs off the porch with my broom.

Clotilde finished with *I don't want to do that anymore.*
The response was overwhelming: Everyone agreed—

No more spiders. *Or bugs!* someone else offered
As a thoughtful addendum that was also applauded.

The senior center volunteer and the senior center Social Director
Tried to calm everyone down, but it didn't work.

Amid all the applause, the staff had their hands full with spilled coffee
And, looking at the clock, pills that needed to be administered.

4

The trick with pills was applesauce, which they had plenty of at hand,
But that only made everyone open their mouths all the more.

The college-student volunteer tried to steer everything back
To the website, but once again nobody quite understood what one was.

Finally, the college-student volunteer's voice became just one more sound
In that large room made small by its crowd of noises.

The residents themselves became the din
Replacing what had previously been the loud TV,

But after a while, by habit and by necessity, one by one
They all nodded off, even with everything so loud.

In that way, the din did what din does, making of itself in this place
A childhood lullaby that held them in its arms, nobody in particular

Waving goodbye to them all as they set off on their ships
Into the deep Thursday water of afternoon dream.

Too Soon Asleep

When dusk falls on us, as it will,
To dim the light of lives outlived,

When night is next, when sleep is sure,
When nothing's left to lift—

I will be glad. The work of a day
Well done, this rest its good reward,

The best we've earned and what
We've won, this doorway opening.

Our lives are like this: years moved on
Beyond the words that started them.

We have sung ourselves as anthem
But the song itself is done.

Good news, though—nice news:
We got through it, beyond it all.

We did not forget the words,
And loud,

So loud we were,
Though we are quiet now.

Leaving without Saying Goodbye

Dying, you've gone ahead, gone before, gone forward—
Without me. I can't find you. But perhaps you are right:

Best not to leave tracks,
No direction, no hint,

Nothing to show that the way might be found
Too easily, that so simply I and so many might follow.

We will, after all, each find a way. It is not cruelty
Not to tell, to stay quiet, to hide so well.

The words we might hear too soon, the magic trick
Explained, so that it is not magic anymore.

Such a simple thing, going away. *Goodbye.*
We say it all the time, this small practice, this

Getting ready, until finally we think we don't have to.
We did not say, but should have, *goodbye* to oranges,

Goodbye to crickets. For all those farewells,
Gone now, they were not enough. We did not learn.

To see you now is to see only part of you.
To see you now is to imagine you, as if you,

My you, are partway submerged in water. I know
Your legs, but I cannot see them now. Those old beasts,

Your feet. Instead, I imagine them. Your legs, your
Hands. But to imagine you is to die a little with you,

To go where you are going, to go as far as I can,
Knowing myself unwelcome for the first time.

I walk with you, anyway, partway into the darkness,
Knowing it's you who will make me turn back.

Open Eye, Closed Eye, Open Eye

After sleep, so simply, a closed eye opens.
The moment is sudden, is all.

What was absent and dark is abruptly full and light,
But then absent again—a blink—a blink

That happens every time, our inside darkness sighing to us:
Don't leave so fast, don't go, please stay.

In that blink-moment we are made to remember,
However briefly, the whole of the night,

The entirety of all nights and all darkness and all dreams
So that a blink is memory, and what memory is made of.

We close our eyes in that moment
But just as quickly open them:

Staying ahead of the darkness,
This feeling quickens the heart.

The Small Secret of Saint Cecilia

My mother was Saint Cecilia,
Saint as best she could be—

This was her confirmation name
And she took it as one of her own.

My mother was Saint Cecilia
When she closed her hands in prayer,

In the confessional,
Maybe one or two other times.

My mother was Saint Cecilia—
But mostly she wasn't,

A little wild, impatient, ready for anything,
In love with candy and the movies.

The name had been the one assigned to her
By the priests at St. Benedict's—

She didn't know enough to ask
Whether they all thought it was really hers.

It seemed improbable given the condition of her knuckles,
So often the cane having landed across them.

And after all, my mother could not sing,
The simple first thing everyone knew about this saint.

She could not sing at all, could not repeat
The Warrington wartime sounds she heard all around her,

A sinister left hand making a full glissando
In the unbreathable air of the blackout-curtained evenings,

The 88th key on the piano down to the first,
This sound the ironic music of the fall of the bombs,

That last note resonant, full of soul-taking
Finality. Another house gone, another neighbor.

Its lyric was loud and its melody plain.
This was the war in England to a young girl

Who could not imagine its end.
The movies and the candy were her small saviors.

But if she could not sing by imitating,
She could sing inside, grace notes in the heart.

My mother was Saint Cecilia most
In these moments.

She sang a song, no matter that it could not be heard—
She sang in her heart and did not stop, could not stop,

In spite of it all, in spite of it all,
Saint Cecilia so simply at her side.

We Play Again, the Great Animal Night and I

Night sky, that freckled, massive creature—
Lively in its crouch above me—

Wants to play. It holds its breath as I look at it,
Night seemingly perfectly still,

Darkness left to birdcall,
Crickets, mothwing, and dogbark.

Night waits for me to go inside the house
So that it can let out its immense breath

Then cleverly change its place,
The whole universe changing its place quietly,

Until I come out again hours later, simply curious
But a player in this great game. I come out

To see whether I can spot the one small star
I saw earlier in the evening.

But I cannot, not quickly, not without effort.
The star has been moved, however slightly,

To the delight of the playful, black beast of sky.
It has won again, easily,

And all I can do is shake my head. *I can move stars,*
It says, and I believe it. I have seen it.

Giants of the Night

You must do this in the very early morning.
The sun must just be rising, the birds

Just starting their first chirps, the world just moving
In its cars and bicycles and distant airplanes.

Walk a little, then watch them emerge—come right out—
The giants that had been hiding inside you.

This is the time of day they come out most fiercely,
Fully confident in revealing themselves,

Feeling loose and smug, protected by the name *shadow,*
Which we call them and so easily laugh off as we point at them.

We laugh and yet there they are, coming out of us,
As if this were normal. Coming out of us. Taller than we are,

Giant beings only vaguely mirror-images of us.
It is daytime, but they belong more to night—

That blackness, which they carry with them as camouflage,
Camouflage or war paint,

So convincing we go right along doing what we were doing:
These shadows belong to dreams, to unlit passageways,

To things we have seen and been scared of in nightmares,
Odd versions of ourselves suddenly disproportionate,

As if they are on stilts, these mockeries of our limitations,
We being smaller than these beasts, and firmer, more rigid.

Sometimes we try, but we cannot catch them.
They wisp through our hands. They cannot be kicked,

Cannot be hurt by rocks, not that we think to try,
At least not since childhood. They are powerful in this way,

In disguise. Invisible, almost. We don't even think about them
After first noticing. Yet, there they are.

They do not move along somewhere else. They do not
Get startled or weary, not any more than we do.

They keep up with us, even when we run.
They are very good at what they do.

How did they fit inside us? How did they unfold
Or steam out of us, or simply emerge? And why now?

These dark shapes, things that look so oddly like us,
To be sure, they were here yesterday and, we think,

They will be here tomorrow.
That might feel like a comfort.

Perhaps it is all simple enough. Occasionally,
We simply look at them—or try—then wonder

Why they seem to look back at us
Exactly the same way we are looking at them.

The Quiet Boy Noé, Who Waited to Speak

He listened, very well.
He could not help himself.

Every sound he heard he remembered,
Making a great library of music inside himself.

He didn't mean to, but could not help himself.
A sound asks for attention, and he gave it.

He stored much of that noise in his head,
But his knuckles cracked some out when he bent them,

And other body parts did the same.
Noé was full to overflowing with what he heard,

And he stored those noises everywhere he could,
Frowning at his noise-leaking knees when he knelt.

When he listened he listened slowly,
And people mistook this for simplemindedness.

But it was the opposite. It was instead
That he took great care to hear,

Something so rare in others
They did not recognize it.

He listened quietly but it was as if he was ravenous,
Taking the sounds of the world in

As if all these sounds were food, meant just for him.
If noise had calories,

He would have been enormous.
And when Noé read, it was slow as well,

Every paragraph a great garden,
Every book a city.

Though they pretended not to,
Those letters, those words, those exclamation points

All made a sound
Just as sure as if they had been whispered.

Through it all, for years, he could not speak.
He could not open his mouth.

It was a fear he had, a certainty,
That if he did, his voice would let go

Something that mattered—not to others,
But to himself, something that fit

The perfect, building concert inside himself
Made by the rest of the sounds at their work.

They filled him, held him up, and to let go of even one
Would be to falter, to stumble.

Instead, quite wisely he felt, he kept quiet,
But this only reinforced what people thought of him.

It was well known that, when asked a question,
He did not answer. People thought the worst.

They could not see inside Noé, hear what was there,
Understand that he could not answer,

That he was at his work all the time,
Sorting through his ears' great harvest—

Clear in his belief
That the world had something very great to say,

And that when he found it, he would say it
And give people their turn to listen.

Three Rivers

1

Late July, and the desert sky has rained this morning.
Running alongside the right bank of the tender river,

Through its wet air, its moist breath, running
Along the loam drifts and sand shore, through

The fallen cottonwood leaves and white seed,
Stepping on the slight twigs, the occasional bones,

Lizard bones, snake bones—twigs as much themselves—
Running along the shallow of this slight river,

A river on an aquifer on a sea, all underneath
Me: I have been here many times, but in running

I am lost, having found this place again
Only in this way, only in this moment.

2

A river to my side, a river underneath,
Two rivers—but a third river, too, when I run.

The humid river I'm inside of—
The slight hint of water I feel on my face,

On my back and legs, soaking through my shirt—
I've run into it, a sailor of this new-risen river,

A rightful citizen of the water.
I am its beast, faster only than the trees and the ants,

Not the frogs. This place, all around me,
It does not keep long on any map:

The river, the water to my left, below, and inside:
This place, this place: I discover it.

Drunk Monsoon

Drunk rain, its big spill, its heavy falling
Out of the chair of sky that held it,

Water slumping down, not able
To keep itself in the sky any longer,

Not able to stand with any attention on the horizon—
Sloppy suddenly, water everywhere,

It simply lets itself go,
A sudden collapse of the thing inside us all

That keeps us upright.
Drunk rain, it comes down not simply as water

But as so much conversation, the way drunk people talk,
A rain that can't stop or help itself,

Talking in fragments, crying but pretending not to,
But crying. Old loves. Moments remembered,

Mouths kissed. Rain, too, was young once,
But this morning it lets go.

This morning it cannot help itself,
Telling us everything.

Seahorse in the Desert

You arrive from the coast in a cloud of dust,
Not a regular horse,

But fast, fast enough to overshoot the shore,
Fast your only explanation,

An exclamation point in the shape of a question mark
At the end of the desert's sentence.

You arrive as the curl in the top of a scorpion's tail,
As one-half the outline of a lightbulb.

Seahorse, you are from another world,
But I see you everywhere. So many of you

Holding up the shower curtain,
That school of you so cleverly hiding—

Having found, and so close to, water,
Bringing to us the spelling of the sea

In that live-body capital *S,*
That handle of every mug,

The slither of every snake.
Unbridled, unsaddled, unshod horse,

One day you will find a way back to the ocean.
This desert, where a great sea once was,

The seaweed turned to tumbleweed,
You have taken it all in stride,

But the salt on your food at dinnertime
Reminds you of home,

Making you restless and keeping you
Kicking in your stall at night.

The Barrel Cactuses of the Northern Sonoran Desert

Stocky cactus after stocky cactus,
Wispy hair and hard spines everywhere,

They are so many drunk men—
Sometimes women, in yellow hats—

Thinking they are standing up straight,
So many thumbs on the side of this hill

All pointing south, hoping to hitch a ride
Across the border, down to the water of the gulf.

It's always about water here,
If only the dream of it. These cactuses,

So many gravestones that have gained weight,
That have filled with the life they bring with them.

So many cookie-cutter houses, in their loose rows,
They are the subdivision suburbia of cactuses.

These porcupines-in-another-life will never be saguaros,
Not thin yuccas or ocotillos, never a tall maguey,

Or happy with so many cousins like the prickly pears,
Who keep adding new additions to make room for everyone.

These barrel beasts bide their time as the less-photographed,
The underfoot, the many-but-invisible,

Grouchy, stubborn, sharp in their opinions,
But with little else in their letters of recommendation.

They are rumored to hold water,
But no Saint Bernard comes here in search of them.

Their water is instead fibrous, just enough,
Carefully guarded. Do not knock on their door.

A House Called Tomorrow

You are not fifteen, or twelve, or seventeen—
You are a hundred wild centuries

And fifteen, bringing with you
In every breath and in every step

Everyone who has come before you,
All the yous that you have been,

The mothers of your mother,
The fathers of your father.

If someone in your family tree was trouble,
A hundred were not:

The bad do not win—not finally,
No matter how loud they are.

We simply would not be here
If that were so.

You are made, fundamentally, from the good.
With this knowledge, you never march alone.

You are the breaking news of the century.
You are the good who has come forward

Through it all, even if so many days
Feel otherwise. But think:

When you as a child learned to speak,
It's not that you didn't know words—

It's that, from the centuries, you knew so many,
And it's hard to choose the words that will be your own.

From those centuries we human beings bring with us
The simple solutions and songs,

The river bridges and star charts and song harmonies
All in service to a simple idea:

That we can make a house called tomorrow.
What we bring, finally, into the new day, every day,

Is ourselves. And that's all we need
To start. That's everything we require to keep going.

Look back only for as long as you must,
Then go forward into the history you will make.

Be good, then better. Write books. Cure disease.
Make us proud. Make yourself proud.

And those who came before you?
When you hear thunder, hear it as their applause.

We Are of a Tribe

We plant seeds in the ground
And dreams in the sky,

Hoping that, someday, the roots of one
Will meet the upstretched limbs of the other.

It has not happened yet.
We share the sky, all of us, the whole world:

Together, we are a tribe of eyes that look upward,
Even as we stand on uncertain ground.

The earth beneath us moves, quiet and wild,
Its boundaries shifting, its muscles wavering.

The dream of sky is indifferent to all this,
Impervious to borders, fences, reservations.

The sky is our common home, the place we all live.
There we are in the world together.

The dream of sky requires no passport.
Blue will not be fenced. Blue will not be a crime.

Look up. Stay awhile. Let your breathing slow.
Know that you always have a home here.

Notes

"Salted Watermelon": I was shocked to learn recently that not everyone grew up salting their watermelon. I still do, and can't imagine any other way to eat it.

"El Trabajo": The names given are not of people known to me, but they are undoubtedly true to the circumstance. So many names have been left in the desert.

"I Do Not Go Away": This poem and others in the collection were first performed as poems, songs, or dialogue in the play *Amexica: Tales from the Fourth World,* which I coauthored with James Garcia. This poem derived entirely from its first two lines, which continue to haunt me in their curious, human truth.

"Immigrant Centuries": Also from *Amexica*. I published a very early version of this unassuming poem, originally titled "Immigrant Times," in the 1970s. Naomi Shihab Nye took it for *Cedar Rock,* which she was then editing. Its simple circumstance remains, but the new temporal reference to "centuries" is a better descriptor and a sadder reality.

"The Cactus That Is My Cactus": I grew up with a tourist sure thing in the shops along the border: lawn pottery and velvet paintings depicting a Mexican peasant in full serape and sombrero with a drooping mustache. It always made those of us who grew up there laugh. Who would lean against a cactus? Tourists, it seemed, would buy anything.

"Legacies": Written for Christine Kajikawa Wilkinson.

"Don't Go into the Library": This poem was included in the 2018 Academy of American Poets' Dear Poet project, although I had been reading it to groups of young readers and in libraries for several years. The poem was featured in talks for the Arizona State University Día de los Niños event and the Arizona Spelling Bee, among others.

"Five Years Later": Written at the request of the *Arizona Republic,* this poem ran as the single commemoration of the five-year mark after the shooting in Tucson of Gabrielle Giffords and others. I've since come to see it as a meditation on suddenness, especially as it has affected friends through the years.

"This Afternoon Explaining about Changing Things": For many years, an older man from Latin America used to visit me in my office to talk about poetry. We sometimes had lunch. He never brought a simple poem; he brought a whole life. Though I could not easily help him with his poems, he made me a better teacher. The poems were bigger than anything I could say about them.

“Even-Keeled and At-Eased”: This is a Golden Shovel poem, a form developed to honor—and use—the work of Gwendolyn Brooks. I wrote this poem remembering that we once sat next to each other on a National Endowment for the Arts panel. The poem is a way of holding the hand of those good conversations once more.

“Industralia”: This poem is one of several in which I use the greguería form—developed by Ramón Gómez de la Serna y Puig around 1910—along with the sonnet sensibility of fourteen lines. The dual form honors my English mother and my Mexican father. I imagine each line as a poem and use the convenience of the sonnet line-count only as a container. These poems are dinner parties for the fourteen invited guests. Two extra guests arrived here unexpectedly.

“At the Recreo and Pitíc”: There’s an old photograph of my father, my brother Tommy, and me leaning against our car, which was parked in the lot behind one of these bars, where they would come out and serve you. In the photograph, an unknown man with a tuba walks past behind us. A party could break out any time in those days.

“Small Detective in a Quiet Kitchen”: Another of the greguería-sonnets, but a double sonnet, as invariably there is much for a detective to consider.

“Faithful Forest”: This poem was written at the behest of the National Park Service and the National Endowment for the Arts. I got to choose a park in Arizona, and immediately imagined I would write about the Grand Canyon. After I thought about it, I realized the Grand Canyon is quite able to take care of itself. The Petrified Forest, which I visited as a young man, seems more of a mystery to the world.

“The Nanas and the Tatas”: I have worked in many senior centers and in medical settings and have a particular fondness for the ten perceived conversations always happening simultaneously. And their length.

“The Small Secret of Saint Cecilia”: This is for my mother, Agnes Fogg Ríos, who passed away February 28, 2016. I miss her. Rara avis.

“A House Called Tomorrow”: This poem is dedicated to my new and first granddaughter, Inés Anita, and to the future she will make as her own.

“We Are of a Tribe”: This is another poem from *Amexica*.

About the Author

Alberto Ríos, Arizona's inaugural poet laureate and a recent chancellor of the Academy of American Poets, was born in Nogales, Arizona, and he has written from that geographical and sociological perspective for five decades. His twelve collections of poetry include *A Small Story about the Sky* and *The Smallest Muscle in the Human Body,* a finalist for the National Book Award. He has also written three short story collections and a memoir, *Capirotada,* about growing up on the Mexican border. Ríos is the host of the PBS program *Art in the 48* and has taught at Arizona State University since 1982.

Poetry is vital to language and living. Since 1972, Copper Canyon Press has published extraordinary poetry from around the world to engage the imaginations and intellects of readers, writers, booksellers, librarians, teachers, students, and donors.

WE ARE GRATEFUL FOR THE MAJOR SUPPORT PROVIDED BY:

THE PAUL G. ALLEN FAMILY FOUNDATION

amazon literary partnership

Anonymous
Jill Baker and Jeffrey Bishop
Anne and Geoffrey Barker
Donna and Matthew Bellew
John Branch
Diana Broze
John R. Cahill
The Beatrice R. and Joseph A. Coleman Foundation Inc.
The Currie Family Fund
Laurie and Oskar Eustis
Mimi Gardner Gates
Gull Industries Inc. on behalf of William True
The Trust of Warren A. Gummow
Carolyn and Robert Hedin
Bruce Kahn
Phil Kovacevich and Eric Wechsler
Lakeside Industries Inc. on behalf of Jeanne Marie Lee
Maureen Lee and Mark Busto
Ellie Mathews and Carl Youngmann as The North Press
Petunia Charitable Fund and adviser Elizabeth Hebert
Gay Phinny
Suzie Rapp and Mark Hamilton
Adam and Lynn Rauch
Emily and Dan Raymond
Jill and Bill Ruckelshaus
Cynthia Sears
Kim and Jeff Seely
Barbara and Charles Wright
Caleb Young as C. Young Creative
The dedicated interns and faithful volunteers of Copper Canyon Press

TO LEARN MORE ABOUT UNDERWRITING COPPER CANYON PRESS TITLES, PLEASE CALL 360-385-4925 EXT. 103

The Chinese character for poetry is made up of two parts:
"word" and "temple."
It also serves as pressmark for Copper Canyon Press.

This book is set in Helvetica Now.
Design by Katy Homans.
Printed on archival-quality paper.